WHAT I'VE LEARNED ABOUT DATING

KEVIN S. CARR

ISBN: 1522947442
ISBN 13: 9781522947448

TABLE OF CONTENTS

AN EXPLANATION

Let me start by telling you why we're here or what got us here I should say. The inception of this book came through a conversation with a friend whom I consider a sister. We were having one of our regular impromptu talks about marriage, dating and everything in between. As we talked and as the wine flowed I soon became the topic of discussion. So here we are on a Saturday night examining my love life and present dating situation. We talked about my past relationships and my hopes for a future one. We discussed my current desire to begin to prepare my life for a marriage and a family. All of which I wish to create and one day walk into. Next up on the topic menu would be dating. With her, being married and "out of the game" as we singles often call it, she was genuinely curious. She was curious about what it was like to date in this current cultural environment. She seemed to be even more curious about what it's like to date as someone who writes and speaks about dating. So I grabbed another slice of pizza, we poured more wine and dove into a very frank dialogue. After about an hour or so, mid conversation she blurts out "you should use this." Noticing the look of perplexity on my face she explains "you need to document this, I really think you should write about your dating experiences as they happen, in real time," she admonished me.

"I don't know," was my immediate reply. I just felt like that would be too personal. Besides, I'm supposed to be the "Dating Expert." "How would it play if I revealed the details of my personal dating process to the world," I thought out loud. Although I wasn't the least bit excited about her suggestion, I obliged and told her I'd think about it. Then I promptly (purposely) forgot her suggestion and went on with my life. Ironically it was some time later as I was researching for another book that I was writing at the time, the one I planned for you to be reading right now that her idea came back to me. This time it struck a chord; here I was immersed in tons of content regarding dating, love, sex etc. when her suggestion became real for me. I finally understood the spirit of her viewpoint as it suddenly became noticeable to me that there is a ton of "expert" advice out there, perhaps too much. What is scarce however, is tried and proven experiential advice. Its one thing to give advice and release content about what you have read or studied, but what I have learned through the writing of this book is that it can be more impactful when you are able to provide a living component to the content that you put out in the world. That's exactly what this is. Not only am I immersed in the topic that is dating I am also currently submerged in the process that is dating as well.

Having written for mediums such as Essence and MSN, I have come to experience that it is fairly easy to get the "expert" label placed on you from everyone from readers to editors. Admittedly it's cool being called an expert at something. It kind of makes you feel warm and tingly inside. Me personally I like to think that I am many things so I prefer to leave the labels up to everyone but myself. No matter what I am called I have devoted the last 10 years and counting to this field in which I am currently engulfed. I have put in well over my 10,000 hours i.e. Malcolm Gladwell. Along the way I've learned that expertise comes from research and practice, but perhaps most importantly it requires extensive experience. So that's what this work consists of; evaluated experience. This book isn't about gender, it's about people and it's for people, just like you and me. Those who have been on both sides of heartbreak and disappointment. Those that want something real, something substantial and are willing to build towards just that.

This book is unlike anything I have ever written before. There are no chapters, only thoughts and moments that I have been able to articulate into what I hope is a clear and concise manner. It reads a bit like a journal, but to be honest I really don't know what it is. That actually may be a good thing as we've already discussed labels aren't always accurate or needed. What I certainly can concede however, is that this is my most personal work to date and that makes me feel liberated and nervous at the same time. Nervous because the thoughts I have put on paper here are essentially a reflection of me at my rawest point. Everything that I have felt during this process, I've documented. The fear, the excitement, the infatuation, the confusion, the disappointment, the inadequacy, the insecurity, the anger, the frustration and even the heartbreak. It's all here. What I've come to realize while piecing together this work is that I needed to write this book just as bad as some of you need to read it. Not that it contains some sort of divine advice to enable you to live happily ever after. Quite the contrary it's full of flaws as is humanity and I believe that's what makes it so powerful. You see what I've learned by dating and writing and writing about my dating is that my experiences aren't so different from yours nor are yours from mine. That makes it relatable and impactful.

I'm learning so much, not just about dating but about myself, about women and about life in general, each lesson shaping me as it comes. I'm also growing at a rate I don't know that I ever have before. I can only contribute that to me learning by doing. I'm learning what I want and what I don't. What works for me and what doesn't. Who fits me and who doesn't. The dots are finally starting to line up in a way that makes me confident about my future and about those desires that I mentioned to you when we first started this conversation. I wish you the same clarity and certainty as you pursue whatever or whoever it is that you're looking for and I hope that you will find my observations valuable. Here's what I'm learning about dating.

VALUES

It seems that we've become a generation that has fallen in love with ideas. The idea of love. The idea of relationships. The idea of success. But until we fall in love with the commitment, loyalty and sometimes painstaking effort that it takes to make all of the above ideas flourish, we'll never realize them. The reason many of us never find that "real thing" or "real one" is because we aren't willing to sacrifice, we aren't willing to be alone for a season, or to hold and keep holding up our standards. We aren't willing to face the fact that the ideas that we have about love and life are only as real as the work we're willing to put in to realize them.

I want passion, but I also want purpose.

I am learning that I want passion but I also want purpose. So the question is what are we planning to do together besides potentially get married, buy a house and have babies? All of these are wonderful things in and of themselves but there's more to life. There's more to my life. I know that there's work for me to do. That's the only reason I'm alive. I've been put here for a purpose and so have you. So as we date and feel each other out let's think about the bigger picture. I'm learning that often we get caught up chasing the allure of a beautiful wedding, a big house, and lovely family. In fact at times we get so caught up that we allow the perception of what we think a good life looks like influence our attachments. I'm learning that for me, at the end of the day, after the wedding and the babies, the accomplishments and the accumulation of all the material things, I need to be able to roll over and look you in the eyes and know that I am here with you, at this moment because I am supposed to be. I'm interested in purpose.

I'm learning the importance of having a picture of what a healthy relationship looks like. I'm also learning the importance of guarding that picture. Many of us start off the race with a limp in that we come from broken relationships. On top of that we turn on the TV or listen to the radio and don't often see or hear a value placed on healthy relationships. Then there are our "friends." I'm learning who to talk to and take advice from and who not to. So many of us take advice from our friends who are in the same broken relationships we're trying to avoid. It's important to find people that represent what you wish to create one day. So I have friends with healthy/faithful marriages. I have friends in great relationships. I make sure to spend time with them. I'm learning the importance of guarding my future in my present because at the end of the day I'm responsible for what I create. I'm learning just because it's trendy doesn't make it true. What do you want your relationship to look like?

You can't share my life if you don't share my values.

I'm learning that infatuation eventually fades and that chemistry can only take a relationship but so far. I'm learning how important it is to live and date according to my values and so that means fist determining what my values are and then engaging with people who share those values. So the question isn't so much if we get along or if they're a nice person, for me the question is, do you value your faith? Do you value marriage? I'm learning that dating people who value what I value makes it easier to decide who actually belongs in my life. This approach helps me keep the big picture in mind and keeps my focus on what really matters when dating. What are your values?

What we produce is a reflection of what we consume.

I'm learning that today matters. Many of us have a desire to be in committed relationships that ultimately lead to healthy marriages. Many of us wish to create healthy and prosperous families, but our current lives, our current way of thinking, our current habits aren't conducive to what we say we want. The TV shows we habitually watch, the music we consistently feed ourselves, although entertaining, and the majority of that content doesn't reflect what we say our desires are. We wonder sometimes why our results aren't different but we don't produce what we want, we produce who we are and we are what we consistently consume. I'm learning the importance of guarding my future today. So if you want to be a great wife or a great husband, it starts now. Right now. Today matters.

Focus on what matters.

We all want someone that we're physically attracted to. That's a given. I know what I like, need and want physically. However, my focus is on what I know will create a lasting bond. Real conversations about the things that make up the best of who we are are intoxicating. Let's move beyond the surface and begin to focus on the things that really matter in our respective lives. If we do this our experiences in dating will change dramatically for the good.

We hear about "happily ever after," but there is no glorification of the work, of the effort that it takes to build something real and because of that our approach has been clouded by unreal expectations of what we think love is supposed to look and feel like. Love is a willingness to choose the same person day after day. It's not about convenience. If you want something real you have to build it with someone who is just as willing to put in the work as you are.

I'm interested in what matters to you.

I'm learning the importance in focusing on what matters most. I want to know who a person is beneath the surface. I'm learning to look pass how they look. I'm also able to ignore their "credentials" which even though enticing at times, still doesn't measure up in the grand scheme of things. As I become more and more acquainted with what matters to me it's imperative that I find out what matters to you. Are you honest with yourself and with me? Do you possess any faith in yourself and in me? Who you are under pressure and stress matters. How you handle disappointment matters. Do you pray and even more importantly do you believe what you pray. That also matters. Looking at what I bring to the table along with yourself, can we now build a house around that table together? Patience matters. Love matters. God matters. Family matters. Vision and purpose matter. All the other stuff is just things that will come in and out of our lives as we journey through it. But they don't matter. We matter and what we have the ability to create matters. So I've decided that when dating my best course of action is to focus on what matters. If I do that my bet is that there will be someone who possesses the same desire to find and indulge in what matters and it is at that place that we'll find each other. What matters to you?

To sum things up...

The thing about values is that we all have them; they make us who we are. Our values are simply the things that we find to be most important in life and our lives tend to tilt in that direction. I'm learning just how important it is to determine what a person's values are. I'm realizing that there have been times where I've misplaced the blame for my wounded heart. It was natural and easy even, to blame the person who had been the object of my affection. However, the truth is they didn't hurt me, at least in the way I thought. I was hurt because I was under the impression that we cared about the same things. I assumed that what I found important, they did too. Values are everything and you can't work around them. You can't build anything significant or healthy with a person with whom you don't share them. The tricky part is that you don't always know what a person values right away. Often it takes time and circumstance for a person to live up to what they really find to be important. I don't know that I have a clear remedy for that fact. I do however have a piece of advice that I've gained from personal experience. There are times when people reveal themselves casually. When they do, don't ignore it. Don't overlook the red flags for the sake of staying on an emotional high.

FACTS OVER FEELINGS

K eep the facts at the forefront and take them exactly for what they are. It feels good to be desired by someone. Feels great when there's a connection that leads to chemistry. Feels good to wake up to a "Good morning" text. These are all good things. However it isn't safe to base your decisions about a person solely on how they make you feel or how you feel when you're around them. I'm sure it feels exhilarating to jump out of an airplane but if I do it without a parachute the results will be detrimental. Feelings can be misleading. What are the facts concerning his/her consistent character? What is on their track record? Do they share similar core values? These are the facts we need to be sure of before deciding to attach ourselves to someone. Embrace the good vibes someone gives you, but just know the facts will help you to determine if those vibes contain enough substance to last over time.

"Man you was who you was 'fore you got here." - Jay Z

One of the biggest lessons I've learned about dating is to take people for exactly who they are. If they have a past or a present that's full of a lack of loyalty, unfaithfulness, and no consistency it won't be any different just because you're in their life. You shouldn't ignore who a person has proven themselves to be up until they've met you. It's not about judging people but it is about guarding your heart and making good decisions in who you attach yourself to. Yes people can and often do change. However I've learned that it's best to let those changes be proven over time before allowing someone in too close.

Don't commit before you're committed and more importantly, before you're committed to.

Infatuation while thrilling provides a false sense of security. It's like an airplane taking us to the heights we yearn for. It feels good and seems safe, so even though we can no longer see the ground we jump! The exhilaration only increases on the way down. Then something happens. Something's missing. Fear creeps in as we realize we've disregarded our safety net. There's nothing to keep us from breaking into pieces. It's in that moment we understand that while infatuation is a joy ride, it's not a parachute and that commitment and consistency are what provide security. But it's too late. We've jumped. The plane is gone and there is nothing to catch us as we have leaped for love at the detriment of our own self.

Show me what you got.

I'm learning to put more stock in a person's consistent actions than their words. Don't tell me, show me and then show me again and again. I believe in guarding your heart and I believe that your guard should only lower in relation to a person's consistent action and effort. I'm learning to allow an individual's consistency or lack thereof to speak for them before I make a decision to invest myself into a situation.

Take advantage of your status. Be tedious in your decisions knowing that you have full control over who gains access to your life.

Use time wisely.

Infatuation is fun but it's fleeting. Consistency and commit-ment are what last and they provide the only foundation that you can use to build something credible. It's OK to ride the wave but you have to manage your emotions a bit and keep an eye on the facts. Don't jump in the ocean without a life jacket. Pace yourself and allow someone's character to come full circle and be proven over time before you give your heart away.

Then there was consistency.

There's something about a person that continues to do the same thing over and over again. Continues to pursue you. Continues to call you. Continues to text you. Continues to articulate his or her feelings for you. The great thing about consistency is that it speaks for itself.

Be Still.

There's something to be said for someone who doesn't have the discipline to simply "be still" for a season. I'm learning that a person's inability to maintain healthy relationships for a sustainable period of time will eventually show up in my relationships with them should I allow myself to go there. I'm learning to pay attention to what I come to know about a person's past as well as to observe their current habits. I'm not willing to ignore the fact that they have a hard time being alone. I won't overlook that they've consistently been in and out of relationships for most of their adult life. It doesn't mean that they're a bad person but it may mean that they lack the emotional maturity to handle my heart and I am unwilling to place my heart in the hands of one who hasn't proven that they are able to care for and nurture it. Some dates will never turn into relationships, and some relationships will inevitably end. That's to be expected but that's not the point here. It's about the frequency in which a person allows themselves to be attached to another without some sort of break in between. It's about the fact that they consistently seem to have the same results and seem to date the same person just in a different body, over and over again. I'm learning that what's best for my heart is to only consider attaching myself to someone who has illustrated the level of maturity necessary to walk in the characteristics that are a representation of what real love is.

FACTS

In the United States only 14.5% of men are six feet or taller. Most of what we see on TV and social media isn't an accurate reflection of the female body type. Some of us have made a habit of dismissing good candidates. There is absolutely nothing wrong with preferences. Trust me I have plenty. But we must understand that there is a difference between settling and being realistic. So he doesn't have a degree, but does he have a proven career or business track record? Does he have a consistent proven work ethic? So she isn't shaped like a coke bottle, does she have a workout habit? Does she take pride in her appearance and take care of her body? So she can't cook, can you? How about you take a cooking class together. Some of us are only single because we seem to be searching for unicorns.

When they're interested they do it when it's convenient. When they're committed they do it all the time. I want that "All the time love."

To sum things up...

A person can only be who they are and I possess no ability or desire to change anyone. What they give me I've decided to take at face value. What they show me habitually I've decided to believe. Consistency, commitment and character will be my guideposts moving forward. I hope that you will be influenced to do the same.

LET'S JUST BE REAL

At times our relationship statuses are only complicated because we allow them to be.

I'm learning that there is no confusion in love and that when it's real, it's also simple. There is no complexity in certainty. At times our relationship statuses are only complicated because we allow them to be. Admittedly, it can be challenging to accept what's right in front of your eyes but that's the only way to grow. One of the character traits that help me in dating is the fact that I am a realist. Either it is or it isn't. Either we are or we aren't. I have lost my desire to entertain the "in between." There's no rush and I absolutely believe that there is a process and progression when dating but I also know that clear communication is the only way to develop something. If a person insists on only giving me "smoke and mirrors" I stop giving them my time. It's simple. Love is simple and it's real.

Can you imagine if we left our comfort zones, lost our pride, got past our egos and just went after the love that we already know exists?

People are famous for saying things like "you shouldn't be looking for love" and "to let it find you." I'm learning that there is absolutely nothing wrong with looking for love when you know what love is. I know exactly what love is, what it is supposed to look like and as a result I have every right to not only look for it, but to expect it especially since I already have a clear point of reference. One of the things that I have come to learn about myself is that I wear my heart on my sleeve in that I tell people exactly how and what I feel, when I feel it. I find that this helps me as it allows me to not only know where I am when dating someone but helps to cultivate a conversation so that I can understand where they are as well. I'm learning that when it comes to what I want, I'm not playing "hide and seek" with my feelings. I don't have time to be staying up late at night trying to determine if you want me or not. Either you do or you don't. I'm fine with either. The more I learn about what love truly is, the more I want it. Not only that, but the easier it is for me to identify those that want the same and those are the ones that I tend to gravitate towards. In terms of your heart I am definitely not advocating negligence I am however encouraging those that are looking for something real, to be just that. Real.

Mutual

Effort isn't based on gender. As a man if I'm interested I'm going to pursue you. I want to, but I also need you as women to let me know that those advances are wanted and warranted. Let's BOTH make our feelings and intentions known. The best relationships are built by two people who are willing to work and build something special together. That starts now. Let's call each other. Let's text each other. It can be so dope when it's mutual across the board.

I desire someone who's real enough to have difficult conversations.

I don't need you to want me per se, but I do need you to know what you want. If for whatever reason what you want changes, I need you to know that to. I also need you to be able to articulate that. I'm learning that our inability to have "difficult" conversations often is what keeps us from being happy. Let's put things on the table. If feelings and desires change then we'll address those things should they occur. I'm learning that there is less confusion and frustration when people are transparent. You can't lose by being real. If you lose someone because they don't like whom you really are, they weren't meant for you anyway and that's not a loss.

Let's go deeper

It isn't enough to "like" somebody. You can "like" a serial killer. I'm learning the importance of being able to identify my core values in another person. I know exactly what makes me happy and I'm very aware of the things that I find most important. So the object is to determine whether one whom I am dating is compatible at the core. That takes time. It requires real conversations, a desire to get beyond the surface and most of all it takes an extreme sense of self awareness. So yes, I may "like" you, but I still need to know more. Let's go deeper.

Transparency is my Super Power

I'm learning that the more transparent I am the less complications I run into. Before you fully engage in the dating process it's important that you know yourself and because I know that I don't have much of a filter I use that to my advantage and I'm often "overly" open with people. I've found it beneficial to be upfront and for the air to be clear. So as much as possible I try to make it apparent as to who I am, what I want and what I'm looking for. I'm also learning to treat people how I want to be treated. I never want to be in a position where I have to constantly guess how someone feels about me. I'm learning that it's very important to find out what works for you. It's important to determine what you value and need and also what you can readily provide without compromising who you are. For me it's transparency. I value it and that's why I give it.

I want you to look at my scars. Not so you can attempt to heal them but so you can see and know that they exist and if after seeing them you still want to be here, then I'll know it's real.

I'm learning that there are different types of people that you'll run into as you go through the process. There are those that will come into your life and they will like some of what they see and then conjure up a list (even if they don't tell you) of what they think should change in order for them to stick around. Then there are those who will see what you bring to the table and they'll choose to sit down and focus on you instead of changing what's on the menu. That's the person that has the potential to stick. I'm not talking about someone that excuses and puts up with all of your bad habits. I'm speaking of someone that knows who you are and wants you anyway. I'm learning that there will be times where we meet people who for whatever reason won't provide what we're looking for. That's to be expected and when that happens I've found it best for someone to make an exit and get exactly what they want. I'm learning that we spend too much time trying to change people into the person we want. The truth is we can't change people. We can love them and encourage them to grow but we can't change them. I'm not speaking of signing up for a situation that you already know you won't be happy in. I'm pretty good at assessing what is or isn't available in a situation and then making a sound decision. I'm also learning that instead of unsuccessfully trying to change people to fit me it's a better use of my time and energy to simply find someone that fits me. I'm also learning that even then, growth will still have to occur from both parties for us to be successful. So my conclusion is that it's better to find someone that wants to, and is willing to grow with you instead of someone who is fixated on trying to change you. That fixation could ultimately prove detrimental to your heart.

To sum things up...

This section is a reflection of multiple moments. In some of them I can recall feeling insecure and unsure about myself and the person I was pursuing. Then there are those other moments, which are also outlined above where I was resolute, defiant even and absolutely certain as to who I am. That's when I felt my best. I was sure of myself, despite anybody else's opinion or perception. It was when I reached this point that I understood what and who I needed to be a part of my life. I only want the one who wants me. That sounds elementary enough but it's actually more complicated then it seems. I've found a lot of people don't want you. They want who they think you should be. That's not the same as wanting who you are. I've decided that for me, in order for me to be satisfied I have to be myself, without exception. I want to reveal all of me and I want someone that loves it. I'll never throw caution to the wind but I have no desire to play cat in mouse. I've grown weary of the grey area. I want to be real, I'm willing to be vulnerable and I long to be open. My search is for someone who feels the same. We all want to be loved in some shape form or fashion. Let's pursue it and even more so let's position our lives to receive it.

INVESTMENT & ATTACHMENT

Be careful who you invest in.

'm learning that sometimes what seems to be self-explanatory gets neglected. I'm learning that a situation(ship) is not the same as a relationship. No matter how much we try to make it so. A relationship is not the same as a marriage. No matter how much we try to make it so. I'm learning to guard my investment. I'm not talking about holding back per se or having an unnecessary wall up. I am referring to what seems to be a mainstream push to convince us that it's OK to invest all of who we are, where there is no commitment. We are often bombarded with images of "couples" who aren't even couples. They're just enjoying the moment I suppose. I've indulged in enough of that behavior to last me a lifetime and as a result I've learned that all of the time that I've spent with people, all of those experiences, regardless if they felt good or not and all of the intimate interactions are non-refundable. I not only can't get them back, I now have to carry the residue of those experiences with me. So I've decided it's best not to give myself to someone prematurely and I have found it more advantageous to line up my level of investment with the level of consistent commitment coming from another person.

No more unnecessary attachments.

I'm learning that sometimes I am my own worst enemy. On far too many occasions we invite people into our lives, and to them, we attach our minds, our hearts and at times our bodies. I'm realizing that I have often invested too much, too freely, too soon. I've created too much unnecessary baggage. Don't get me wrong, as I have no regrets but I do realize the ramifications of my actions up until this point. Most of us have a desired end. Whether that's a marriage or simply a healthy committed relationship. The problem is that as we travel through life to our desired destination we tend to make too many pit stops. Not only do we make pit stops, but we also pick up passengers that don't add anything at all of value to our respective journeys. If a lot of us are being honest we'd admit, we don't need another person to miss, another experience to have to get over, or another sexual relationship to remember and unfortunately have to try and suppress so we can attempt to take as clean of a slate as possible into where we ultimately want to be. I'm learning to enjoy the moment and not to live for it because what or who I allow into my life today will undoubtedly attach itself to my tomorrow.

Some lessons can be avoided.

Some lessons can be avoided. Just like school, you aren't required to learn everything to keep moving forward, just what's necessary and everything isn't necessary. Yes, it's true that there have been times where we have confused a lesson for a soulmate. However in many cases it is also true that if we were a bit more intentional we would've realized that we had no business in that relationship at all and wouldn't have needed to learn the lesson that it consequently brought about. I'm learning to be very intentional in the dating process. Although there is a chance that I may grow as a result of experiencing heartbreak, I'm learning that my ability to avoid those situations altogether serve as a sign of growth. Simply put I'm learning not to lend someone the hammer that will eventually be used to break my heart. I'm learning to stay intentional.

Why fight to stay where you aren't wanted, needed or desired?

I'm learning that there is really no use in fighting to stay where I'm not wanted, needed or desired. I'm learning that sometimes people do you a favor by letting you go and that sometimes rejection is a blessing because you can't get to the place that you ultimately want to be until you leave where you are. Some of us are our own worst enemies. We punish ourselves by continuing to pursue people who whether it is through word or action have shown us that they don't want us. At least not in a way that's healthy and or sincere and beyond surface. So when someone turns to give you a push out the door, allow it to be a boost as you head to where you really want to be, a place where you are valued.

You reap where you sow.

Think about the stock market. An investor gathers information and studies the track record of a potential investment before deciding to move forward. This allows him or her to forecast a bit and take a calculated risk. Dating is no different. Monitor a person's consistency and gather all the information you need to make clear choices in which you should be attached to. Relationships only flourish if you cultivate them and that takes time, effort and consistency. Be sure to only invest yourself where there is clarity and certainty.

You don't get to choose your place in my life.

I'm learning that people love to be in your life on their terms. I had to stop and remind myself one day that this is MY life. I control who comes in and out of my life and for how long they get to stay. I won't allow anyone else to dictate that for me. At the end of the day if there is no reciprocity. If you can't or are unwilling to give what I'm willing to give. If you are intent on staying in an emotional cage and refuse to meet me at a place of vulnerability then we may just need other people. I'm learning to be OK when those types of situations occur. I no longer have the energy to entertain people that only want to go half way and do just enough. I'm in no rush nor am I into pressuring people to see what I see and want what I want. I'm just at peace with the realization that though it may not be the person that I thought it would be, there is someone out there that sees value in reciprocity, in relationship and is willing to build everything that they say they desire.

Let's be crazy about each other.

I'm learning that more and more people are becoming hesitant to put their cards on the table. Many of us are afraid to feel something for someone, not realizing that there is no weakness to be found in opening your heart. Only the courageous among us are willing to do so. The culture around us in large part has become a dream killer to those of us that still believe in the power of love. I'm learning not to let my optimism or my desire to be downsized. I am determined not to settle until I find what I know is available. Passion. Fire. It's not about a fairytale. Quite the contrary, love is very real. I'm learning that I need someone to feel for me what I feel for them. Someone that loves with the same intensity in which I am capable loving. They may show it and articulate it differently but the passion will be the same. I've had plenty of lukewarm experiences. If you aren't on fire for me there is no need for us to come together and try to build something that will ultimately crumble because only one of us wants it passionately. Yes I want someone to be logical, and purposeful. All of those things are greatly needed and expected. But I also need someone who "feels" it. Whose heart is invested? No pride, no fear and no reservations. I want to be crazy for you and you for me. Let's be crazy for each other.

To sum things up...

All of what you just read is dedicated to anyone who has ever invested themselves into someone who didn't deserve it. It's dedicated to those of us who've allowed far too many unnecessary attachments, yet somehow we're still here. It's dedicated to the fighters, and to the resilient. It's dedicated to you. It's not about the past, the future is where our focus should be. So in that vein let me say this; from this point forward make a promise to yourself that you won't invest in anyone who is unwillingly to invest in you. Promise that you won't give your heart to anyone who hasn't first proven both a desire and an ability to care for it. Promise that you will only attach yourself to those that add value to your life. If you do this, you'll be better for it. I can say that confidently because I've made the same promises to myself, and it's the best thing I could've ever done.

BUILD WHAT YOU WANT

Please understand that my decisions concerning you are purposeful not personal.

'm learning that I'm building my life day by day and step by step. It's a journey and each of us have our own course and perhaps more importantly our own rhythm. It's because of this that each of us needs a partner that moves at a pace that's complimentary. I'm learning that everyone won't recognize the song of your life. Some will, and yet even some of them still aren't suitable to dance with you. The dating process is teaching me that a great pairing requires intention and for me to be deliberate but it also requires a natural fit. That means that the details do matter. I'm learning that not only am I interested in building a relationship I also need for that relationship to be a partnership as well, because there is also a life we will need to build together. So just like the businesses and dreams that each of us is striving to create our hearts also require the same diligence. I'm learning that my dating decisions should be more purposeful than personal.

I've finally figured out why it's so hard for you to tell me the truth, you're too busy lying to yourself.

I'm learning that the truth is the starting point. I'm learning that far too many of us have no idea of who we are or what we really want and so we just keep attaching ourselves to people and convincing them to entangle themselves in our own insecurities and lack of self-awareness and then blaming them for not being what we think we want or wanted. I'm learning that I owe it to those I date to be sure of myself. To know what I want. To know what I can handle. To have an idea of where I'm going. To have settled what I believe. I owe it to them to be self-sufficient and not expect them to make me whole or provide the answers that I should already have. I'm learning that the reason many of us never find what we're looking for is because we have no idea of what that is. I'm learning that until I am capable of identifying what my truth is I'll always be incapable of articulating that to someone else and as a result I'll just hurt those interested in me and continue to come up short of what could be the best thing for me. The truth starts with me. It starts with you.

Great Expectations.

I'm learning that if you expect nothing, you tend to get just that. Why wouldn't I place expectations on someone who is seeking entry into my life? I concede that expecting the person you've been engaging with for a week to turn into a great spouse because of a few funny text messages is a bit unrealistic. But I'm learning that expecting loyalty, clear communication and commitment are all beyond valid. I'm learning that your expectations should come from your desires. I'm learning not to let people, social media, or any other outside influence convince me to dumb down my desires and my expectations. I know exactly what I'm looking for and I expect to get it. As should you. Keep dating and most of all keep expecting!

Are you interested in commitment?

Interest is a great start but at some point I need it to develop into commitment because that's what it takes for things to grow. I'm also learning that a person's willingness to commit says a lot about them. It says that they're decisive; it says that they're willing to invest in something besides themselves. It also says that they have the sense of certainty that's needed to develop and maintain trust. I know that things take time to grow, but I'm learning that it's best not to waste my life on people who are only excited about being interested and not about being committed.

Goals > Trends

Just like anything in life, goals are necessary. They also should be specific and have substance. I'm learning that relationship goals have to be more than us just sitting courtside at the game or being cuddled up at the beach. Those are awesome experiences but none of that really matters in the overall scheme of things. What matters is what kind of life we can produce together. Can we build a family that we both can be proud of? We like each other but do our respective lifestyles even mesh? Are our relationship goals even the same? And so my focus during the dating process is to determine if we can walk through life together. I'm learning that relationship goals aren't the same as relationship trends and I want my relationship to be an accurate reflection of my goals not of what's popular at the moment.

Let's be intimate.

You have to first dig in order to build. Surface interactions produce surface relationships, if they produce relationships at all. I'm learning the importance of two people understanding the value of being able to be intimate without any physical interaction. I'm learning that the best parts of whom I am come out when I'm willing to dig deep and let someone see what I'm really made of. I'm also learning that everyone won't be interested in this level of communication and some just won't be capable of it and that's Ok. There's a natural exclusivity that comes with intimacy. Probably because the type of intimacy I am referring to first requires a certain level of trust and comfort and that takes time. I'm learning that those who aren't capable of opening up are one of two things, they're either uncomfortable with me or they're uncomfortable with themselves. In either instance we wouldn't be able to produce what I'm interested in. I see people every day that I'm sure it would be fun to have sex with, but I've had plenty of sex. It's rare that I find someone that I want to be intimate with. I'm learning that's where the treasure is. Let's go treasure hunting.

You have to build what you want.

I'm slowly but surely learning not to fall into the comparison trap. So often, even when we find ourselves in relationships we want to be in different relationships. Perhaps with the same people but we want them to look and feel how culture tells us they should. For others of us we feel like whether it is due to our age, our means or pressure from other outside factors, we should be further along in terms of our relationship status. Maybe we should. Who's to say? But I refuse to undermine my happiness by discounting where I currently am just because a future I haven't even reached yet seems more appealing. I understand that the future has to be built. Step by step. Brick by brick and as much as we may want it to come ready-made, it doesn't. If it did how would we grow? How would we be able to build a relationship that's unique to what we want? I'm learning that in life, in business and especially in relationships no matter where you find yourself, you have to be willing to build what you want. If not, you'll always end up sabotaging your own happiness by chasing what you will never receive because the truth is; you only get what you have put in the work to create.

To sum things up...

I used to think I would one day meet someone who would complete me. I had it all mapped out. They would be everything I needed and wanted. They would look a certain way, act a certain way and dress a certain way. I always assumed that the woman of my dreams would simply be a carbon copy of the one that I had created (along with the help of social media, music videos and the church, yes even the church) in my head. I believed we would meet and we would have this amazing relationship and life together. Maybe we will to some extent but what I now understand is that it won't just happen because I want it to. We will have to build it and so above all those other things, her appearance, her background, her faith and career track I need someone who I can build with. We are all different and we should be and we all need different things at different stages of life. Wherever you may find yourself today I hope that you realize that you will have to build what you want and I hope that you find someone who understands the same.

DECISIONS

There comes a time when "I don't know" is no longer an acceptable answer. I'm learning that people will try to hold you hostage with their indecisiveness and then get mad at you because you're unwilling to put up with their inability to make a decision. Sometimes you have to tell people to shoot their shot or pass the ball. Time is precious and I don't have a moment to waste treading water in the "grey area." If after all of that they're still are unable to make a decision about a future that includes you, and then guess what? At that point their non-decision whether they realize it or not, is a decision. I'm learning that sometimes you just have to accept that and keep it moving.

An ultimatum is just an expectation with a deadline.

Some people will try to convince you that there's something wrong with giving them an ultimatum. There isn't. I'm learning that you absolutely have the right to want to see and be able to measure progress in whatever situation you may find yourself in. An ultimatum isn't always voiced. At least not with words. There are times when enough is enough and you will have to decide if you're going to stick around and remain unsatisfied or be courageous enough to change the way you interact with the person who's either incapable or unwilling to provide you with what you're looking for. You may have begun with expectations and if over a reasonable course of time those expectations have yet to be met then you may have to draw a line in the sand and spell out your needs for the immediate future in ALL CAPS.

There's power in choosing someone out of the crowd.

I'm learning that there is power in being decisive and in making a choice. I've gone through seasons in life where I relished in having options. So I went around accumulating options and talking about all the options I had like they amounted to a badge of honor. I'm learning that options are cool for a time but there is something that opens up for you when you make a choice. Actually choosing someone and then deciding to choose them over and over again every day. That's real substance and that's what love is about. I'm also learning that before you make a choice first understand that you are responsible for that choice, so it's up to each of us to choose wisely.

To sum things up...

Always allow someone the space to choose, and when they do never begrudge their choice. It can be a challenge to accept when someone doesn't choose to see you in the way that you see them, but where there is decisiveness there is clarity and that's what you need to move forward and produce what it is that will satisfy your desires.

RIGHT PERSON
RIGHT TIME
RIGHT FIT

There's power in someone's willingness to love the reality of you.

One of the hardest things you can do is also often one of most beneficial, and that is to give someone freedom to choose. It takes a certain level of security within yourself to just be whoever you are and open your life up so people can decide if they want to be a part of it. It's a challenge, it's scary and even often frustrating but it's one of the best things you can do. I've learned not to force myself on people because love begins with a decision. I'm learning that decision is best when made without my direct influence. We all have the desire to be loved and to be loved for who we are. There's power in someone's willingness to love the reality of you. It is because of that, that I've chosen to indulge in the reality of who I am and to allow people to see me, for me. I'll be a different person a year from now. Hopefully we all will. But when we talk about love, about commitment and choice, I desire for someone to want ME not an idea of me that they have conjured up because I only put my good cards on the table. Love requires a bit of a leap. Everyone won't jump for you, and everyone isn't meant to. It isn't their fault or yours. But the person that does dive into the deep end will do so because they know and have weighed the risk and have chosen to choose you regardless. That's what love is about. So be who you are at all times, unapologetically and enthusiastically YOU.

What you provide is exactly what someone is looking for, don't change, and don't fall into insecurity. Know that some- one needs and will respond to exactly who you are.

Sometimes you don't get who you want.

I'm learning that sometimes you don't get who you want. It could be due to bad timing, a conflicting lifestyle, or another person's preference that you just don't appear to represent. The reality is every connection doesn't blossom into something that lasts forever. But every good and purposeful connection made will produce memories, lessons and moments that you can treasure, so carry them with you as you go through life minus the person you thought you couldn't live without. You can and you will. It will take a bit of time to get over the disappointment but as you keep living you'll soon see that it all matters and that everything happens for a reason, even the heartbreak that you were so sure you'd avoid this time. Don't be ashamed to go through your process. Allow yourself to feel what you feel. But don't let your heart become sour. Don't give up on love or yourself. I know you've been waiting and wanting, but stay patient. Stay open for exactly what's yours. I'm learning not to take life so personal that I become jaded about what's possible. You will like again. You will love again and you will get to the point where you want and need someone that wants and needs you just the same. Stay encouraged.

A lot of people get caught up in projecting what they think the person they're getting to know will find attractive and intriguing. I've learned the best course of action is to be explicitly myself and allow people to see exactly what my life and lifestyle consists of so we both can make accurate decisions about whether or not we are a good fit for each other. Why start off trying to force a puzzle piece that clearly doesn't mesh with the whole puzzle?

You shouldn't have to change who you are so your relationship can work.

Many times we meet great people that aren't necessarily meant to be in our lives romantically, but because we're afraid we won't find anyone better we try to force things. If people don't fit. They don't fit. The right person will compliment you and enhance your lifestyle not hinder it.

Sometimes you have to cut people off.
Cold Turkey.
No Explanation.
No phone calls.
No texts.
No emails.
No more replies.
Just be done.

Sometimes you develop great relationships with people that may transform into other things even if not in a romantic way. Then there are those times when that's not the case. Some people just want to linger in your life to see if they can get something from you without having to invest in you. It's important to know when the latter is happening and someone just doesn't have good intentions. Everything isn't meant last forever. I'm learning that some people and some relationships, even when good are just for a season and when that season has ended so should that relationship and all that it entails. Stay Free.

To sum things up...

Everyone isn't for you, even the ones you like. Everyone doesn't fit even the ones you want. No matter how much we try, we can't control the timing of life. All we can do is live, love, and be ready to receive what we've been looking for.

STAY SECURE

Let's turn excitement into certainty.

I don't want to be one of those people who's always excited but never certain. Admittedly I am one who loves "the chase" and the excitement that comes with it, but as I grow I'm learning that certainty is more important to me. Granted there are very few things in this life that are certain. But I'm learning to be absolutely sure about who I am, where I am, what I want and who I want at any given moment. I'm learning that it's good to have people who you're excited about but it's even better to have people in your life that you're certain about. I'm also learning to have less and less time for those that are unsure of themselves because I am beginning to understand that it takes a level of certainty to build a healthy relationship. I'm also learning to stay away from those who make me feel uncertain about where I stand with them. Life's too short to have to convince someone that you're good for them. The truth is maybe you are. But the fact that they aren't sure of themselves or you means that they aren't good for you. Stay where you're secure.

There's nothing wrong with you.

I'm learning that there is nothing wrong with me. There is nothing wrong with you. I'm learning that people like to try and "mold" you. There are bound to be times where you will engage with people and throughout the course of your relationship you will develop (good) habits you've never had before, you will see things in ways that you never have before. That's exactly what's supposed to happen when you meet good people. Iron sharpens iron. What's not supposed to happen is someone insisting that you change because they're comfortable with who you are. We've all been told at times we're too emotional, too sensitive, too serious or too much of something. I refuse to fall into the trap of blaming myself for someone else's inability to grow up and grab on to a good thing. I'm not too much. I'm me and I'm just enough for the person that needs, wants and fits me. That may not be you and I'm OK with that.

I won't let you practice on me.

Some people aren't ready for what you're ready for, but because they don't want to be alone they'll offer half of what you need hoping that it's enough to convince you to stay. This isn't practice and "life is not a dress rehearsal." I want what I want and you're in ability to measure up to it doesn't change that. I'm a fan of blatant honesty. I try to provide that as best as I can and that's what I expect in return. I don't need you to be where I am, however, I do need you to be honest about where you are. I can respect honesty. I appreciate candor. What I can't tolerate is someone just looking to buy time because they want the comforts that come with intimacy while they're trying to figure things out. If you don't know yourself, you don't need to know me.

You do realize you'll never meet another me right.

I'm learning that sometimes you have to feel yourself and realize that you are the only YOU on this earth. So it isn't arrogant to realize that your time, energy and commitment is precious and that whoever receives it is privileged. I'm learning that you shouldn't have to convince someone that you're special. If they can't see it, maybe they aren't supposed to. There are many things worth fighting for in this world, but someone's attention isn't one of them.

I'm glad that your thoughts about me are not my thoughts about me.

I'm learning that people will just naturally develop their own thoughts about me and that's their prerogative. That doesn't mean I have to accept their view of who I am as my identity. We've all been told we're too much of something or not enough of something else, at times by people who we wished desired us as we did them. I'm learning not to take those things personal and not to allow their perception of who they think I am hinder who I actually am. Too fat, too needy, too emotional. Not this. Not that. No degree. Too many kids out of wedlock. All those opinions will cripple you if you let them. I'm learning it's important to be whoever it is that you are at this very moment. You should never have to apologize for not being who somebody else thinks you should be. The right person won't want you to be anybody else; they won't desire you to bring anything else to the table except for what you bring. Be you. Be free and stay proud of who you are.

Suppose you became the person you were looking for.

I'm learning that I've spent too much time "searching." At times I've allowed myself to get caught up looking for this sometimes (mythical) person that I thought would suit me. As I'm growing I'm beginning to understand that it's more important for me to ensure that I am the person that I am looking for. What I mean is this: The more I date and engage with people the more I learn about myself. What I've come to realize is that who I sit across from at dinner consistently is just a mirror of who I already am. A lot of us get so upset with our results and rightly so that we begin to change our approach to dating, we make adjustments to our mental "checklist" on what we need in a mate. We assume all of this will ensure that we come across the right person. Unfortunately it doesn't, because we've changed everything but ourselves. So here's what I'm learning, everything that I say I want in another person I need to already possess. Ironically as I focus on myself I see that some of the things that were on my "checklist" we're only there because they were deficiencias of mine. Now that I'm addressing them I don't need another person for that. What I need is to already possess every quality and attribute that I say is important to me because if I don't, I'll never find them in another. You only get what you bring to the table, no more, no less.

Let's play for keeps or not at all.

Admittedly, I haven't been in a lot of serious relationships. I've gone through phases where I've desired everything but commitment and I've also had my moments where commitment was at the top of my agenda. Through it all what I've learned, is that I take relationships very seriously. I'm learning that it takes a tedious thought process when dating to create the relationship you desire. I'm learning that relationships flourish best in the midst of certainty. I'm learning that when I remind myself of the power that comes with two people intentionally deciding to create something together my thoughts about dating are totally different. I'm more intentional. I'm more open and focused. I'm more willing to be patient and engage in the process. The more thought I put into my relationship now, even while single, the better chances of me creating and living out exactly what I am looking for. So don't feel bad for being picky, for not committing to just anybody. It's your heart and your life. Take it seriously.

I'm learning not to take everything so personal. I'm also learning that sometimes what we think is rejection isn't rejection at all. Just because you aren't good for someone doesn't mean you aren't "good." It's not always an indictment on you. The fact that it's only one you mean that you are unique and it will require a unique individual to get and keep you. So don't be discouraged and don't give up on the dating process. I'm sure you have and will continue to come across people who want you but soon you'll find someone who needs you, all of you and that's powerful. That's what we're all looking for isn't it? Stay on your journey and keep smiling.

Happy isn't what you feel. It's what you are.

I'm learning that I have often made the mistake of searching for someone who could potentially make me happy. The truth is if you're not happy then you won't be happy, and it doesn't matter who comes into your life. There will be times when you meet people that speak to the best parts of you and bring some semblance of sunshine into your life. However, that's more about you than it is about them. I'm learning to not just ride the emotional waves that the feelings of happiness often produce; I'm learning how to just be happy no matter what.

It's not me, it is you.

As cliché as it sounds there is actually truth in the old adage, "it's not you, it's me." One of the most important lessons I'm learning about dating and about life in general is that there is never a good enough reason to beat yourself up. I think at times we all have to get over the temptation to indulge in self-pity just because someone doesn't see us as we want them to. I'm learning that isn't my fault or error, it's theirs. I'm learning each day to give myself the credit I deserve. It's so liberating when you reach the point where despite of what anybody else says or does or thinks, you know that you are enough. I'm learning that when it comes to my experiences, my disappointments and even my shortcomings, though I do have to carry them with me I also have two choices. I can allow them to pull me or push me and I for one prefer the boost. So if someone wants to leave, let them. If someone continues to overlook you, let them. Don't fight for anyone's attention. Don't diminish who are and don't allow the shade from others to dim your light. Stay secure.

You could be just one "Hello" away from everything you want in life. Don't be discouraged because of a bad experience with someone who wasn't for you anyway.

To sum things up...

I think it's hard for some of us to understand that we aren't to blame. Not for the relationships that didn't work, not for the things that didn't go our way and not for the people who did not live up to whom we wanted and expected them to be. No matter how tempted we are to beat ourselves up when we're disappointed, we must remember it's not our fault. We owe it to ourselves to be secure, knowing that who we are is enough and it always has been.

BE WILLING TO LET GO

I'm not worried about you.

I'm learning that there is no logic in worrying. It does me no good and it's counterproductive. Many of us spend too much time worrying and not enough time living. We're worried the person who we're with won't stay. We're worried that the one we want won't want us the same way once they realize who we really are. We're worried that we won't find the person who we think we need in the time frame we think we need them. We're worried that we'll be single for longer than we desire. We're just worried. Those are all very valid concerns, but worrying will do nothing to change the future, it will only ruin our experience in the present and it also hampers our ability to be "present." I'm learning that the latter is especially harmful because it takes us to be present to find what we're looking for and it is our insistence on worrying about the future that hinders our ability to see the good that's right in front of us. Yes, I will remain open, and continue to take initiative and pursue what and who I want, but what I won't do is sacrifice my sanity or my inner peace worrying about what is beyond my control.

I'm not afraid to lose you.

I'm learning that not wanting to lose someone and being afraid to lose them isn't the same thing. Fear blinds our ability to see clearly and make healthy decisions when it comes to our hearts. The fear of losing someone often makes us compromise in an effort to keep an individual who doesn't want to be kept. I'm learning that my best experiences when dating have been when I've allowed myself to be in a position of wanting someone while simultaneously being OK if they didn't want me in the same way or with the same intensity. There's freedom in that vulnerable place. There's power in knowing that you'll get exactly what's for you. Too often we give our power away because we're afraid to be without a particular person not recognizing that at times our willingness to let people leave is the best thing you can do for them and for you. Often it is in our willingness to be without that we gain everything we want.

I'm learning that you can't be afraid to let go. Also, I'm learning that you do yourself a disservice when you become so prideful that you can't handle being let go of. Sometimes it just doesn't fit. When you know what you want and more importantly what you need, consequently you know when it is or isn't available. It's best that you date accordingly and not waste your or anyone else's precious time trying to force yourself into a situation that doesn't supply what you're looking for just because you're tired of being single. I'm learning to end things that need to end by remembering that with every ending comes a chance to begin again.

Bye.

That one little word can save you a world of frustration and at the same time open you up to a whole new world of possibilities. Be brave enough not to explain your progress.

To sum things up...

At your lowest moments, your strength is often found in your willingness to let go.

WHAT I LEARNED FROM WOMEN

f she's taking her time, it's because she probably needs it. During that time, be consistent, be real and be transparent. While you wait, contemplate, pray, and develop a plan. Make sure you know who you are and that you identify your purpose because you'll need it. Prepare yourself for life with her. Prepare yourself for what you say you want and if she ever opens up fully and decides to give you her heart, know that it was after much deliberation. Know that with it comes great responsibility. Know that all this time even though you thought you were waiting for her, she was waiting for you.

It's simple. If you can't be consistent then don't ask for her attention. If you're not ready for something beyond the surface then don't try to monopolize her time. If you want to be single then stay single. Don't lead her to believe that she's the only one. If you're not willing to pursue her, then leave her be. Don't start what you can't finish. If you aren't ready to open up, don't expect her to. If you don't understand what love is, do her a favor and find out before you try to grab hold of her heart. It's not complicated, just be real.

A few good dates don't deserve a standing ovation, consistent interest fuels consistent effort.

To pursue a woman has nothing to do with calling or texting her daily. It's bigger than taking her on dates. To pursue her means to be honest. To be consistent. To become vulnerable and to articulate your feelings for her every step of the way. It means to reveal your intentions. To make sure she knows you want her and only her and that you remind her often. Extend as much effort as you can and then extend some more. To pursue a women means that you alter your life in such a way that it's facing not only her but the future you see with her. If you've done that. You've done your job.

She's only expecting you to be who you said you were in the first place. That's more than reasonable. She doesn't want anything more than what you offered her in the beginning; she just wants you to offer it consistently. That's fair. She's often patient with your lack of urgency when it comes to commitment. That's admirable. She wants you to respect her time, her mind and her body. When you think about it she just wants what any human being desires. Reciprocity.

Until you can offer her that, don't offer her anything.

Articulate your feelings but don't talk so much that all you do is "talk." Your intentions will be confirmed by your consistency. Stop trying to force yourself on her, just be who you say you are and allow her space to make a sound decision.

Don't make her feel bad for pursuing other options when you don't have any intention on being the only option.

Don't chastise her for being hesitant. It's probably an instinct she developed along the way in order to protect herself from men who have approached her in the same vein as you. With the same gestures and similar promises. Even if you're different you'll have to prove it. Understand you weren't the first one to reach for her heart. If you are who you say you are and want what you say you want, it will show in your patience. That requires humility but your long suffering will provide for her a clear picture of what love is and that's all she wants to see.

You only deserve what you work for. So don't bombard her with expectations that don't match your effort, and then get upset when she doesn't comply with your request. If she's strong enough to be resolute within herself and not follow you around haphazardly she's exactly what you need. But she won't come easy. Don't allow your insecurity to impede her ability to choose, even if it isn't you. Real love begins with a choice. You want something real right? But please understand that you don't get chosen just for showing up.

Having to win her affection never went out of style.

She's not your mother nor is she bound to your well-being. Leave your request at the door. If she does anything for you, it's out of the goodness of her heart, so respect it but don't expect it. She doesn't owe you a thing. There's nothing free in this world. Either step up to the plate or invest in what you say you want or save her the frustration that will undoubtedly accompany your unwillingness to put in a little work.

Stop telling her she's intimidating. She's not. What she is, is sure of herself. She's clear about what she wants and she's certain about where she's going. That's exactly what you need whether you realize it or not. What you feel isn't intimidation; it's the light of her awareness shining on your insecurity. Don't blame her.

Maybe she isn't "yours." Maybe her heart doesn't belong to you and maybe it never will. Maybe you were only meant to be there for a season. Maybe God wanted to use you to be a new picture, a change of pace or a step in the right direction. Maybe it was part of your purpose to love her so she could know what love is. Maybe you are what she needed in this moment in life to be equipped for what is in store for her. Maybe you were just a vessel to get her ready. Do you know the humility that takes? If you can be trusted with that, take pleasure because you can be trusted with anything.

Don't insinuate that you want intimacy and then complain about her emotions. They come with it. Don't deter her from being passionate after you've light the fuse within her heart. Don't try and convince her that she's complicated when you're the one who keeps going back and forth. If you would say what you mean, mean what you say and do what you've said you wouldn't have to answer so many questions. Of course she's inquisitive, she wants clarity. If you can't provide her with that then do her a favor and disappear. She'll be able to see then.

To sum things up...

To be honest most of what you've read in this section were notes that I essentially wrote to myself. The others were to the men who have yet to learn what it means to actually pursue a woman. The ones who are arrogant, self-serving, and far too often pretentious. We have to get to get it together. I say we because I've been there. It isn't hard to be. Especially for a black man. If you've made it beyond 25 and you have a college degree, a functional career or business, no criminal record and no children, you are a rare minority. The bad part is, you know it and that knowledge arms you with a sense of entitlement. That can not only be frustrating to the women who are willing to open up themselves to us, it's also counterproductive to what many of us one day wish to produce. Fortunately I've been able to re-discover what a joy it can be to pursue a woman wholeheartedly. I hope that more men would do the same. I've always thought that one day I would meet a woman who made me want to love her the way she truly deserved to be loved. I have since dismissed such thoughts. I now realize it to be my absolute duty to become such a man that will rise to the level of responsibility required to genuinely love a woman. It is on me to multiply her joy, help her live, make her laugh and most of all provoke her to love without regret.

It's a Journey

'm learning the importance of knowing exactly where it is I'm going and what that place looks like for me. I'm learning that many times we get blinded by looking for a wife or a husband when it's not really about that. It's about knowing your desired end more than anything. That could be a marriage or it could be a long-term committed relationship. Only you know the future you see and desire. So it's not really looking for a person, it's more of moving toward a place or a goal. In doing that I'm noticing that your life will change as well as your interactions while dating. Your approach and even your conversations will change. When you know where you're going you also become aware of who can go with you. I'm learning that many times the reason we attach ourselves to the wrong people is because we're looking for people in the capacity that we think best serves us. I'm learning the solution is to focus on where you wish to be and in doing that, it will make it much easier to identify the person best equipped to take the journey with you. They'll be equipped because they're interested in going to the same place as you. I'm learning that this approach could save us tons of unnecessary heartbreak. Cheers to the journey.

Drive Slow.

I'm realizing how important it is to pace yourself and recognize that if a relationship is going to develop it's best to let it do so in stages and through seasons. Sometimes after a few good interactions with someone we're tempted to push all of our cards into the middle of the table. I'm not saying hold back. I am saying it's important to let time do its job. There will be instances where you won't have to do anything but be patient and time will tell you everything you need to know about a person or a situation. Sometimes it's just best to be still and not rush to the future.

Sometimes it's trial and error. Just remember that one good or bad encounter will not make or break your desired outcome. It's going to be a series of steps, a series of dates, and a series of conversations. It takes time to build something significant with someone significant. I'm learning to not let my impatience short cut the process.

To sum things up...

You know what really changed my life and even altered my approach to dating? It was when I settled within myself that I have a long life ahead of me. More days, more months, more years. Think about that, there are so many possibilities that life offers us as we live. I understand some will rebuttal my optimism by admonishing me that tomorrow isn't promised. I guess that's true, if you believe it to be so. But who really wants to die tomorrow? Let's focus on the journey and come to grips with the fact that good things take time. That mindset helps me when I'm disappointed and aids me in not giving in to depression. It also fuels me to keep moving knowing that although I may have not secured all of what I want yet. It's still out there and it's still mine. I pray for your strength and that you will embrace the journey and that instead of worrying about life, you would live it.

THE FUTURE IS BRIGHT

Don't limit your expectations to your past experiences.

I am more than what I have experienced and there's more to be experienced. It's easy to become jaded by what didn't work as well as become infatuated and stuck on what did. In both cases we tend to carry those experiences around with us looking for and expecting the same things we've already experienced, but this time with different people. I'm learning that both of these approaches hinder my ability to create a healthy relationship. We've all been hurt before, some more than others. We've all "played the fool," some more than others. We've also all had some really good experiences with good people. The key isn't to forget your past, but to understand that there's more out there and that no matter how bad or good your relationships have been there's still better ahead. I'm learning that the only way to grow is to first expect it. So as I focus on harnessing my expectations my goal is not to limit them by only entertaining people who provide what I've become accustomed to. Some of us do that far too often. We've become so used to being treated a certain type of way, that we're comfortable with it and every situation we get ourselves into provides that same type of comfort even if it isn't healthy for us or what we ultimately want. I'm working on changing the way I think about myself and my future and as a result I can sense the bar being raised on my expectations.

You will be disappointed.

I'm learning that just as with anything in life there will be times when you will be disappointed. People may not turn out to be who you thought they were. A relationship may not develop with someone you're interested in. Things don't always work how we think they should. But I'm learning that they always work out how they're supposed to. So I'm choosing to focus on life's possibilities not its disappointments. This keeps me from becoming jaded to the point where I start to believe that every person, every date, every relationship will be the same. It won't. Just as each moment is different so is each experience. So keep living. Keep moving. Keep meeting and engaging. Stay open and keep dating. Don't lose your optimism knowing that it's on the journey that you find what you need and what you're looking for.

Circles are important.

Here's the thing about circles, they are inclusive. The experiences and people who are in our circles form a pattern of life. That pattern which is full of habits, ideals and perceptions continually repeats itself. If we aren't careful we will allow our respective experiences to trick us into believing that life doesn't have anything else to offer. When the truth is, it is our circle that is limited. The facts show that there are plenty of good quality single men and women to go around. Even if they aren't in your circle. So we have to allow ourselves to grow, to meet new people, explore different places and then we will have the opportunity to make new connections and experience new things.

It's Ok to be disappointed; it's not Ok to stay disappointed. Allow every broken connection with the person that wasn't for you to fuel your fire for the one who is.

Sometimes the people we want only exist to show us the people we need.

I know you thought they were "the one." They weren't and that's Ok. They were just another piece to the puzzle that is designed to help you grow. There is someone out there who loves with the same intensity as you do. There's someone who shares your desire for loyalty and reciprocity. Someone who values not only commitment but the work that it takes to make a relationship flourish. Don't be discouraged and don't give up. Nothing comes easy, not even the love you desire.

You will love again.

Throughout this entire process I've learned so much that I almost feel like I've been in school. My greatest and most poignant lesson has been that the experiences that I have articulated in the previous pages aren't exclusive to me. Though my thoughts are personal and my feelings my own there's a corporate context that lies within every moment that I've documented. Without a doubt I know that what I've felt has been felt before and the places where my emotions have often led me are more crowded than I could've imagined. That's proof that though there are times when it feels like it, we're never alone. Neither you nor I. It is my hope that this book does for you what it has done for me. I've grown tremendously and I'm grateful for where I presently am. I know what I want and more importantly I know what I need. I'm optimistic about what's to come. I'm open to new connections and I'm more encouraged than ever before. Everything that I've experienced and subsequently written about has lead me here.

Of course there's more to learn and more to life, but there is a peace that comes with knowing that it's a journey and though each of our paths are different what we experience along them, not so much. So take heart and know that with each passing day we have the potential to get better at life and as we do everything else gets better as well. Including our dating experiences. Cheers to the journey.

I wish you the very best,

Kevin S. Carr

P.S.

I hope that you have enjoyed this conversation but it isn't meant to end here. In fact I'm already preparing for our next one. Until then, if you've gotten anything at all out of the preceding pages please share this book with someone else. Remember our experiences aren't our own. Buy someone a copy, give them your copy or point them to where they can get their own copy. Whatever we need to do to amplify what we have just collectively experienced, let's do it. Just don't keep it to yourself.

Remember…

Love is worth everything it costs. Don't settle.

Made in the USA
Columbia, SC
31 March 2019